Picture the Past

Life in a New England Mill Town

Sally Senzell Isaacs

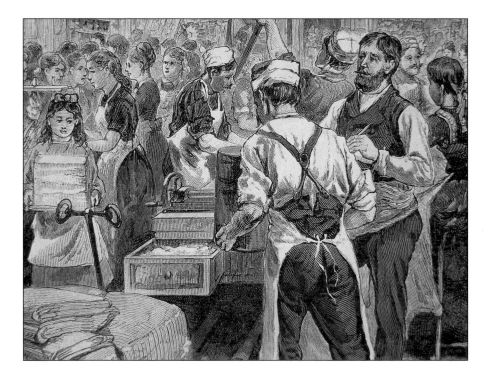

Heinemann Library
Chicago, Illinois

© 2003 Reed Educational & Professional Publishing
Published by Heinemann Library,
an imprint of Reed Educational & Professional Publishing,
Chicago, IL
Customer Service 888-454-2279
Visit our website at www.heinemannlibrary.com

Produced for Heinemann Library by
   Bender Richardson White.
Editor: Lionel Bender
Designer and Media Conversion: Ben White
Picture Researcher: Cathy Stastny
Production Controller: Kim Richardson

07 06 05 04 03
10 9 8 7 6 5 4 3 2 1

Printed and bound in the United States by
   Lake Book Manufacturing, Inc.

Library of Congress Cataloging-in-Publication Data.
Isaacs, Sally Senzell, 1950-
   Life in a New England mill town / Sally Senzell Isaacs.
      p. cm. -- (Picture the past)
Includes index.
Summary: An overview of life in a nineteenth-century town
in which most people worked in the textile mill, including
their housing, food, clothing, schools, and everyday
activities.
   ISBN 1-58810-693-4 (HC), 1-40340-525-5 (Pbk)
   1. Lowell (Mass.)--Social life and customs--19th century--
Juvenile literature. 2. Lowell (Mass.)--Economic conditions--
19th century--Juvenile literature. 3. Textile industry--
Massachusetts--Lowell--History--19th century--Juvenile
literature. 4. Textile workers--Massachusetts--Lowell--Social
life and customs--19th century--Juvenile literature. 5.
Northeastern States--Social life and customs--19th century--
Juvenile literature. 6. Northeastern States--Economic
conditions--19th century--Juvenile literature. 7. Textile
industry--Northeastern States--History--19th century--Juvenile
literature. 8. Textile workers--Northeastern States--Social life
and customs--19th century--Juvenile literature. (1.Lowell
(Mass.)--Social life and customs--19th century. 2. Lowell
(Mass.)--Economic conditions--19th century. 3. Textile
workers. 4. Northeastern States--Social life and customs--
19th century. 5. Northeastern States--Economic conditions--
19th century.) I. Title.
   F74.L9 I86 2002
   974.4'4--dc21
                              2002000794

Special thanks to Angela McHaney Brown at Heinemann Library
for editorial and design guidance and direction. Thanks, too, to
Martha Mayo, Director of the Center of Lowell History, for help in
supplying images for reproduction in the book.

Acknowledgments
The producers and publishers are grateful to the following for
permission to reproduce copyright material: Center for Lowell
History: pages 14, 26. Corbis Images: Bettman Archive, page15;
Mark E. Gibson, page 30. Library of Congress: page 25. North
Wind Pictures: pages 3, 7, 8, 12, 20, 22. Peter Newark'sAmerican
Pictures: pages 1, 6, 13, 16. Lowell Historical Society: pages 10,11,
17, 27, 28, 29. University of Massachusetts, Lowell: pages 9, 18,19,
24. Cover photograph: Lowell Historical Society.

Every effort has been made to contact copyright holders of any
material reproduced in this book. Omissions will be rectified in
subsequent printings if notice is given to the publisher.

Illustrations on pages 4, 21, 23 by John James.
Map by Stefan Chabluk.

ABOUT THIS BOOK

This book tells about daily life in early mill towns in the United States from the years 1800 to 1900. A mill, or factory, is a building where something is made in large numbers with the help of machines. Looking mostly at Lowell, Massachusetts, this book presents the history of **textile** mill towns in New England. In the early 1800s, the textile mills in Lowell had more workers and made more cotton cloth than any other city or town in the United States.

We have illustrated the book with photographs taken in the first mill towns. We have also included artists' drawings of how people lived at that time.

The Author
Sally Senzell Isaacs is a professional writer and editor of nonfiction books for children. She graduated from Indiana University, earning a B.S. degree in Education with majors in American History and Sociology. Sally Senzell Isaacs has written more than 30 history books for children.

Note to the Reader
Some words are shown in bold, **like this.** You can find out what they mean by looking in the glossary.

CONTENTS

Making Things Faster

In 1789, American women made cloth at home. They usually started with sheep's wool. They used a wooden wheel to spin the wool into yarn. Then they would **weave** the yarn into cloth using a small, wooden **loom.**

At the same time, England had mills with machines that could spin yarn and weave cloth much faster. Samuel Slater worked in one of those mills. He memorized all the parts of the spinning frame. Then he came to the United States and built one. Slater opened the first U.S. **textile** mill in Pawtucket, Rhode Island.

Look for these
The illustration of boy and girl mill workers shows you the subject of each double-page story in the book.

The illustration of a mill marks boxes with interesting facts about life in a mill town.

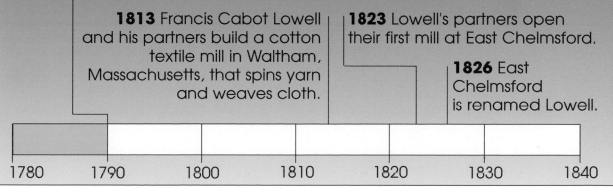

TIMELINE OF EVENTS IN NEW ENGLAND'S FIRST MILL TOWNS

1790 Samuel Slater starts the first cotton mill in Pawtucket, Rhode Island. Its spinning frames make cotton yarn.

1813 Francis Cabot Lowell and his partners build a cotton textile mill in Waltham, Massachusetts, that spins yarn and weaves cloth.

1823 Lowell's partners open their first mill at East Chelmsford.

1826 East Chelmsford is renamed Lowell.

1780   1790   1800   1810   1820   1830   1840

The earliest mills were built on rivers, near waterfalls. They used the natural power of the rushing water. This map shows the United States around 1870.

1840–1870 Over 7 million **immigrants** come to the United States from Europe. Many find jobs in mills and factories.

1844 Samuel Morse opens the world's first **telegraph** line.

1876 Alexander Graham Bell makes the first telephone call.

| 1840 | 1850 | 1860 | 1870 | 1880 | 1900 | 1910 |

More Mills

Francis Cabot Lowell lived in Boston. He traveled to England and visited **textile** mills. English mill owners were afraid people would copy their new machines. So no one was allowed to take notes while inside their mills. Lowell tried to remember everything he saw. When he returned to Boston, he asked his family and friends to help him start a new business **weaving** cotton cloth.

These machines are called power **looms.** They weave yarn into cloth. A wheel under the mill turns the gears and belts of the looms on the upper floors.

Lowell built a mill by the waterfalls on the Charles River in Waltham, Massachusetts. It was the first mill with machines to spin yarn and weave cloth in one building.

Early mills were mostly made of wood. From about 1820, mills were made of brick and had several floors. This is Boott Mills in Lowell as it looked in 1852.

WORKING IN THE UNITED STATES

In 1800, most Americans worked on farms. Over the next 100 years, people moved from the farms to cities to get jobs there.

- Working in mills and factories (New England)
- Fishing and whale hunting (New England states)
- **Coal mining** (Pennsylvania)
- Building railroads (midwestern and western states).

A Mill Town

Soon the mills in Waltham were turning out enough cotton cloth to make 6,000 shirts a week. The owners looked for a new place to build larger mills. East Chelmsford, Massachusetts, seemed perfect. It was next to the powerful Pawtucket Falls on the Merrimack River.

Francis Lowell died in 1817. In 1826, the town of East Chelmsford was renamed Lowell in his honor. This is how Lowell looked as a city in 1836.

These five young women moved to Lowell to work in textile mills. They lived together in a **boardinghouse.**

Who would work in the new **textile** mills? Only a few farm families lived nearby. The people in charge of the mills sent workers to farms in several states to offer jobs to the daughters of the farmers. The young women moved to mill towns to work in the textile mills. They earned money to spend on themselves or to send home to help their families.

Houses

In 1830, most of the workers in Lowell **textile** mills were young women between the ages of 15 and 30. They were called "Mill Girls." These unmarried women lived together in **boardinghouses.** An older woman cooked for them and made sure they were safe.

This is a row of ten boardinghouses in Lowell. About twenty young women usually lived in each house. There were many bedrooms. Four to six young women shared each bedroom.

As early as the 1830s, Lowell boardinghouses had cold running water. They did not have hot running water. The toilets were in attached "outhouses." Many workers' houses in New England were the same way. The people in charge of a mill made much more money than the workers. Those people and their families lived in large houses owned by the mill companies.

The large houses of people in charge of a mill had nice gardens, and **servants** worked there.

LAWRENCE HOUSE.

Adults at Work

By 1850, many Americans were leaving their farms and moving to towns to work in factories. People earned more money in factories. In the factories, the windows were closed all winter. The air was often stuffy, and the machines were very noisy.

Mill Girls worked the **looms** in the **textile** mills in Lowell. The power looms in a mill **weave** yarn into cotton cloth. The cloth is sold all over the world.

In 1845, a Mill Girl earned about $16 a month. Today that would be about $2,000 a month. Men earned almost twice as much as women. Everyone worked six days a week.

On the farms, people worked from sun up to sundown. In cities and mill towns, the factory bells told people when to go to work and when to go home. Farmers did many different jobs in a day. Factory workers usually spent the day doing one job.

A TYPICAL WORK DAY

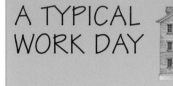

4:45 A.M. Factory bells to wake up

5:05 A.M. Bells to start work

7:00–7:30 A.M. Bells to go home for breakfast

12:30 to 1:05 P.M. Bells to go home for "dinner" (largest meal)

6:45 P.M. Bells to leave work

7:00 P.M. Eat "supper"

8:00 P.M. Visit, write letters, sew, read

10:00 P.M. All visitors must leave the **boardinghouse.**

13

Children at Work

When Samuel Slater opened the first U.S. factory in 1790, he had nine workers. They were all children between the ages of seven and twelve. Slater soon decided adults would be better workers. By the 1880s, new **immigrants** and poor families needed their children's wages to help pay for food and rent.

The picture on this five-dollar bill shows children at work in a **textile** mill. The paper money was specially made for a bank in Lowell.

This young girl changed the bobbins on a spinning frame. A textile mill was a dangerous place. Workers had to be careful. Fingers or clothing could get caught in the machines. Children and adults sometimes got hurt.

Children worked in all kinds of factories. They were especially good in the textile mills. With their small fingers, they could change **bobbins.** They also could clean small parts of the machines.

CHILDREN'S JOBS IN THE 1800s

Coal mines
Some children picked stones out of the coal. Others smeared grease on the coal car wheels to make them run smoothly.

Textile mills
Children watched the yarn spin onto the bobbins. When bobbins were full, children replaced them with empty bobbins. They sometimes kept the yarn straight as it spun or tied broken threads.

Canning factory
Children packed empty cans with fish or fruit as machines moved the cans along.

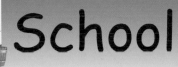

School

In the 1820s, schools were built in Lowell for the children of the mill workers. In most parts of the country, African American children were not allowed to go to school with white children. In Lowell, all children attended schools together.

Teachers were strict in those days. They were even allowed to hit a student who did not behave.

Children learned reading, writing, history, and math in school. In the early years, each student brought his or her own books from home. After 1832, the school provided the same books to all the students.

This is the inside of the Dover Street School in Lowell. The photograph was taken in 1897.

Many people were worried about the children working in the mills. The state of Massachusetts passed laws to keep children out of the mills and in school.

1836 Children under fifteen could not work unless they attended school the year before.

1852 Children between the ages of eight and fourteen must attend school at least twelve weeks a year.

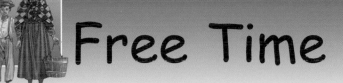

Free Time

Mill Girls worked six days a week. When they were not working, they enjoyed their free time. There were music concerts, dances, picnics, and plays. There were classes to take, shops to visit, and train rides to Boston. Reading was also popular.

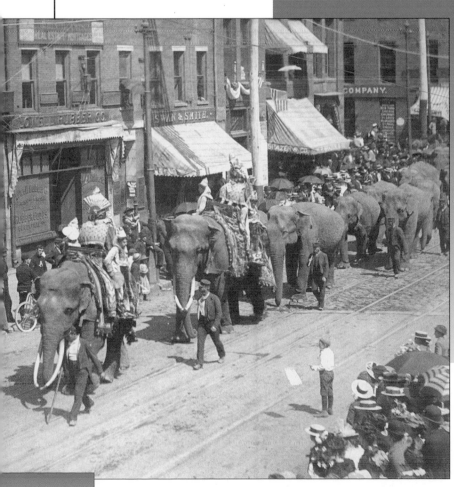

As it did every year, in 1893 the Barnum and Bailey Circus came to Lowell. The circus traveled by train from city to city across the United States. When it arrived, the animals and performers paraded down the main street.

Many Mill Girls enjoyed shopping. In the 1840s, a pair of shoes cost about $1.10, which equals $175 today. A hat cost $1.50, which equals $260 today. Besides going to stores, people bought things from **peddlers** who came to the house. Peddlers sold books, shoes, perfume, and candy.

Actors came to Lowell to perform plays. This poster advertises a funny play called "Grist to Our Mill!"

LIBERTY HALL.

FOR A FEW WEEKS.

Wm. F. JOHNSON - - - - - - - MANAGER
W. H. CURTIS - - - - - - - STAGE DIRECTOR

GREAT NOVELTY! PARLOR COMEDY!

GREAT SUCCESS!

COMEDY TRIUMPHANT!

MONDAY & TUESDAY EVENINGS, JUNE 16 & 17, 1851,

Will be acted Planche's Elegant Comedy in 2 acts, of

GRIST TO OUR MILL!

MARQUIS DE RICHVILLE, a Miser,..........................Mr W. F. JOHNSON
MONS. DE MERLUCHET..........................Mr W H. CURTIS
Prince de Conti..........Mr Joyce | Old Butler..........Mr Leighton
Theiry du Mont ....Mr Howe | Madmoiselle de Merluchet.....Mrs Rainforth

With the money they made, Mill Girls could buy a couple of pretty dresses. They also bought a hat, coat, and combs for their hair. They kept their dresses clean by covering them with aprons. They wore their hair pulled back so it would not get caught in the machines.

After the cloth left the **textile** mills, it was shipped to other factories. There, women sewed the cloth into dresses and men's suits.

By the 1870s, U.S. factories were making clothing of all kinds. Many people were buying clothes from stores rather than making them at home. When men wanted to look stylish, they wore black silk top hats and long, fitted coats. Women wore long dresses that sometimes had a large bow at the back. They also wore hats.

In 1876, people came to look at the new **steam engine** on display in Philadelphia. People wore the types of clothes they would wear to a picnic or a fair.

Food and Cooking

The Mill Girls ate all their meals at the **boardinghouse.** For breakfast, they ate pancakes, oatmeal, or eggs. At noon, they were given 45 minutes to go home, eat dinner, and return to work. A typical dinner included meat, potatoes, other vegetables, and pudding or pie for dessert. After work, they ate a lighter meal that they called "supper."

This is the kitchen of a rich person, possibly an owner of a large factory. **Servants** are making a large meal. The iron stove was invented in the early 1800s. Before then, people cooked in fireplaces.

Mill Town Recipe—Apple Cobbler

There were many fruit orchards on the farms near Lowell. In the summer and fall, farmers delivered fresh apples, pears, peaches, and vegetables to the boardinghouses. The woman in charge of the house kept the food in the cellar where it was always cool.

YOU WILL NEED
1 cup flour
2 teaspoons baking powder
3/4 cup sugar
1/2 cup brown sugar
3/4 cup milk
1/4 cup butter
2 cups sliced apples
2 teaspoons cinnamon

WARNING: Do not cook anything unless there is an adult to help you. Always ask an adult to use the mixer, the knives, and the oven, and to handle hot food.

FOLLOW THE STEPS

1. Preheat the oven to 325 degrees Fahrenheit (165 degrees Celsius).
2. Melt the butter. Pour it into a 9 x 9-inch (23 x 23-centimeter) pan.

3. Measure the sugar, brown sugar, flour, baking powder, and milk, and pour them into a mixing bowl. Blend them together well with a mixer to make a smooth batter.
4. Pour the batter over the butter in the baking dish.
5. Sprinkle cinnamon over the apple slices. Place the apple slices on top of the batter in the pan. Do not stir.
6. Bake for one hour in the center of the oven. Serve warm.

This recipe makes 4 to 6 servings.

Getting News

In 1835, a newspaper cost a penny. Lowell had several newspapers. A typical paper had advertisements on the front page along with a short, enjoyable story. The next pages had news about Lowell and other places in the United States and the world.

24

LOWELL AND THE TELEPHONE

- Alexander Graham Bell, the inventor of the telephone, visited Lowell in 1876 to show people how the telephone worked.
- In 1879, Lowell was the first U.S. city to use telephone numbers. Instead of telling an operator, "Connect me to Mr. Jones," they told the operator the telephone number.
- In 1879, the first telephone line set up between two cities was between Lowell and Boston.

After 1844, Lowell and other cities had telegraph offices for sending important messages. A person gave a message to a telegraph operator. The operator put the message into a clicking code. With a special machine, they sent the code through telegraph wires. An operator in another city listened to the clicking code and wrote down the message.

This is a telegraph operator. In the background are a steamboat, steam train, and a steam-driven printing press. All these inventions helped news to travel faster.

Transportation

In the early 1800s, **canals** were important to the mill towns. Lowell's main transportation canal was the Middlesex Canal. Soon, the **textile** companies needed faster forms of transportation than canals could offer. The owners of the textile companies built railroads. Trains and **trolleys** became a major form of transportation in mill towns.

People used horse-drawn boats to carry passengers and supplies along the Middlesex Canal. It went from Boston to Chelmsford, Massachusetts.

Most workers lived near the mills so that they could walk to work. People traveled further across town by horse-drawn wagons. By the 1840s, they could ride trains to Boston and other cities.

These people are taking a trolley from Lowell. They will spend the day at the ocean.

Factory Changes

Beginning in the 1840s, **immigrants** came to the United States looking for jobs in the mills and factories. By 1860, immigrant women were working in the Lowell **textile** mills.

By 1900, cities had grown all over the country. New factories were built in these cities. Instead of water power, these new factories used coal-powered engines. Later they used electricity.

In the late 1840s, a disease killed Ireland's potato plants. More than a million starving Irish people came to the United States. Many of these immigrants went to work in New England mill towns.

Many factories were not safe places. There was little fresh air, the work was dangerous, and people worked long hours. By the late 1800s, workers formed groups, called **unions.** The unions told factory owners to pay workers more and to make factories safer. If the owners refused, the workers stopped working. This was called a **strike.** Many strikes were unsuccessful, but the unions did make factories safer places to work.

These are the workers of Boott Mills in Lowell. The mill opened in 1835 and closed 120 years later in 1955.

Mills Today

Over the years, most New England **textile** mills moved to the South. Later, many of them moved to other countries. Many of the Lowell textile mills have closed, but their history is not forgotten. In 1978, the Lowell National Historical Park opened.

Today, visitors to Lowell can walk through a museum filled with power **looms.** They can take a trolley, ride in a **canal** boat, and visit a **boardinghouse.**

Glossary

boardinghouse place to live where meals are provided

bobbin large, wooden spool that holds yarn for making cloth

canal body of water made by people. A canal connects one body of water to another.

coal mine place where coal is taken from the ground. Coal is burned to heat water and power machines.

immigrant person who moves from one country to live in another

loom machine used to weave yarn into cloth

peddler person who travels around selling things

servant person who works in another person's house

steam engine machine that uses steam for power

strike to stop work to make a point

telegraph machine that sends messages in the form of a clicking code from one place to another over lines

textile cloth made by weaving or knitting

trolley car that runs on tracks in the street. Its power comes from electric wires above it.

union group of workers who join together to help improve things

weave to make cotton or wool cloth by passing yarn over and under each other

More Books to Read

Isaacs, Sally Senzell. *America in the Time of Abraham Lincoln: The Story of Our Nation from Coast to Coast, from 1815 to 1869.* Chicago: Heinemann Library, 1999.

Isaacs, Sally Senzell. *America in the Time of Lewis and Clark: The Story of Our Nation from Coast to Coast, from 1801 to 1850.* Chicago: Heinemann Library, 1998.

Isaacs, Sally Senzell. *Life in America's First Cities.* Chicago: Heinemann Library, 2000.

Index